LAND LEGS

CELINA SURESH

To Jody, Attiqah and Elaine:

For showing me a kindness so rare,
Every day since by fate we met,
A single dedication of love falls short,
So I give you these three. Thank you.

CONTENTS

ACT III: SADNESS

INTRODUCTION

I've thought long and hard of this moment - when my work goes out into the world for the first time. What do I hope to achieve? Who am I doing this for?

I grappled with these questions for a long time, guilt and shame churning inside. I wondered if it was as simple as wanting my work to be seen by others or as complex as wanting to achieve one of my life's goals as a poet. Shame quickly took its shot at these, echoing what I'd heard my whole life - that my role was not to shine and I will always be a failure. It had always been impressed on me that writing poetry was a nice hobby, a private outlet. But all of these couldn't be farther from the truth.

Poetry had started for me as a sort of purging. As my voice was silenced over the years, I found such comfort in a form of writing where I could use little words to convey deep wounds. Living in the chaos of trauma, I also feared the quiet when demons I couldn't see came alive in my mind. Poetry became the faithful companion that sat and talked me through the terrors.

Years later, I had lost hope of ever having a life without pain and was fantasising nightly of finding peace through death. This was the only constant feeling I'd had throughout my life. But something changed when I realised my 30th birthday was coming up.

I'd told myself years ago just to hold on till this year because at least then I could say I had given it my best shot. I wasn't afraid of death, a companion as much as poetry had been all this time. But thinking of turning 30, I suddenly felt incomplete - like I wasn't finished yet, like my story wasn't over.

I didn't understand those feelings. I was drowning in pain, numbing myself every night with alcohol. It had to be time. But - big but - I couldn't help thinking about those feelings. I wanted to know what else was there… and I did have a couple of months left. When I started therapy for the third time in my life, it was with the vague hope that I might be able to "live" instead of just "survive". My new therapist said I might even "thrive" - I scoffed.

As we started our sessions, my ever-faithful companion, poetry, nudged me along. We processed traumatic memories, long-buried pain and intense emotions; we moved through the chaos by finding definitions, seeing connections and placing meaning; we discovered a voice, a narrative, a person - my inner child.

She looked so small - malnourished, filthy and petrified as she was. I spent many of my quiet moments coaxing her to talk to me and tell me her story. My heart broke again and again as I felt her pain, her anger and her misery. I wanted more than anything to find the courage that she had all these years to never give up and this time, to use it to tell her story.

And I want to thank every single one of you for listening to it.

ACT I: PAIN

"Silence about trauma also leads to death - the death of the soul. Silence reinforces the godforsaken isolation of trauma. Being able to say aloud to another human being [what happened to you]... is a sign that healing can begin."

- Bessel van der Kolk, The Body Keeps the Score: Brain, Mind, and Body in the Healing of Trauma

The Sea

The sea churns restlessly,
For deep at its centre it holds the pain of many,
It reaches up to those teetering on its surface,
To toss them about recklessly, for it hurts to bear this burden.

I know of no other surface but this.
The waters had been shallower when life had started,
But as she grew into her domination and they remained in their
neglect,
The breeze swelled into a gale and pushed me out further.

By now my sea legs have strengthened.
I marvel at this now-old rickety boat that's held me for years,
Through the terrifying gusts of control demanded from her,
And the blame, dismissal from them, that were somehow more
frightening.

It seemed to appear suddenly out of the horizon -
A gleaming sailboat, a man standing tall at its bow.
Promises of love and protection were sent as a lifeboat,
I scrambled quickly out of their boat to reach for his.

An image of the knight from my dreams,
I'm immediately swept along in the tales of romance.
I am told to never look into his boat,
My young vulnerable mind doesn't question my saviour.

But the darkness slowly showed itself as the days went on.
It had always been around my boat just out of sight,
Waiting for the opportune moment to appear to me,
When the winds from my family had put me at my worst.

There is no pretense after my sixteenth -
Once the law was lifted, so was his self-imposed control.
He smirks with satisfaction as he drags me deep within,
Where no one can hear the cries of my humiliation.

Time has passed and I stand adept through yet another storm.
My spirit and body have deadened.
The storm rages on all three fronts - from her, them, him.
There is no fight in my eyes, my soul never stops screaming.

Just as my spirit has accepted its fate,
I see a boy of my age drifting nearby in a yacht.
My mind awakens slowly, wondering,
And hope sparks in my heart.

It is no easy feat but every day I hide to watch the boy.
I envy that no storms seem to touch his boat,
My soul yearns to know what it is like just to drift,
I silently start to plan.

It happens on a day planned by my heart,
When rage coursed through his fingers to crush my throat.
Unbeknownst to even myself, my spirit had been ready to leave and
Without a fight from my body, he accepts there is no more love to
exploit.

I step off his boat and drop straight into the sea.
Shocked, I flail about shouting to the boy to save me.
He peers from his yacht and smiles with empty comfort,
But never reaches his hand to lift me in.

Fear abounds. But as I cling to the side I am also relieved,
For while I flounder about in the raging open seas,
I have found an odd sort of freedom -
Trapped in no one's boats, I can now build my own.

And so I do – plank by plank, nail by nail.
Through the turbulence of the winds and seas,
Through the pains of rejection,
Though I long to give up, I never do.

It is years later when I have finally built my raft.
I push away, comforting as it has been to have hung on,
And paddle towards a mirage of green and brown,
The storms starting to lighten the closer I get.

It is land I have seen as the sands of the beach twinkle at me,
But I catch sight also of my family - beckoning me forward.
My body freezes but the waves continue to nudge me forward,
For it had deemed it my time to leave its chaos.

I take a step onto the solid ground and immediately collapse.
My legs, having stood adroit on the stormy seas,
Have no experience on this unmoving surface.
I look up still crouched, unable to comprehend of a world that
remains still.

I see familiar faces stop to gawk at my fallen position,
I'm confused at their stares, wondering if they'll extend a hand,
My family stride over, forcefully hauling me up,
Shoving the last piece into their perfect family portrait.

In case you're wondering, no hand ever came.
As I had learnt on my own the skill of surviving on the seas,
As I had learnt to build my own while enduring the hurricanes,
I learnt on my own to stand still and even walk steadily inland.

It was the sea that had held the bottomless pit of my pain for years,
The sea that had borne every storm that came my way without
breaking under me,
The sea that had guided me towards the land when the time was right
for me,
And so I always look to the sea to remind myself of strength and
resilience.

It's That Moment

At first you were shocked
Appalled at their behaviour
Your system shuddered
But only the slightest fear crept in

Then you were comforted
Looking at them smile and love
Just a slight misunderstanding
You felt for them

Then it happened again
This time your eyes stayed on them
And you saw something flicker on their faces -
Was that hatred?

They're smiling again
What's happening to them, to me?
They say it's what I did
How could I have angered them?

This time it's longer
My legs give out, terrified
My arms ache, raised for too long
My body bows, its only defense

They're watching me, waiting
I'm trying so hard
Not to move, not to speak
Then just one slips through.

I didn't mean it, I'm sorry
I knew better, I'm sorry
I'll do better, I'm sorry
I deserve this, I'm sorry

I was good, I swear
I didn't say a word, not one
I didn't disrespect, not once
It's me, I realise.

I walk through the door prepared,
My face void of any thought or feeling,
My body tensed for the slightest movement,
My punishment for existing.

When it comes I drop, knowing my legs will buckle,
My arms move to the back of my neck, to shield,
My limbs gather toward my torso, to protect,
I wait patiently, as they exhaust themselves.

One last kick, disgusted at my passivity,
One last insult, hatred still pumping through,
One last glance, annoyed it wasn't enough,
One last time? Never.

I am disgusted, ashamed
I hate myself, more than they do
I am terrified, there is no escape
I am nothing, there is no escape.

Neglect

Alone and rejected
I hurt you by being defective
It doesn't matter that it was them
Who damaged me
I must be strong enough
To rise above everything
Because I look awful
Everyone can now see

You turned to him
Away from me
His reality of me is true
Mine can never be
I am alone
Out here there's no one
A child deserted
Where are her protectors?

I don't understand
Help me be better
The world is crushing
I cannot breathe
Why won't you look at me
Why won't you see my pain
Alone in the darkness
I sink further into this black hole – to protect your image

The Silent Dream

She sat by a closed window
Hopeful eyes raised to the moon
Its soft beam caressing her face gently
As she dreamed a silent dream

Skipping down the lane
Seeing a bright future ahead of her
The past seemed redundant
The present full of surprises

Suddenly she stopped
Her eyes full of tears she turned back
The past was coming alive
When she looked ahead
Her dreams had vanished

Where there was once hope
Unbelievable sadness filled her young heart
Silently, so no one could hear her
She whispered,
"I used to dream a silent dream".

Dear Little One

Dear little one,
I see your tears flood every night in grief,
For a lost sister, a violent rejection,
How could you have understood.

Dear little one,
I see you reach out desperately,
For love, for attention, for a hint of concern,
But to no avail, your family turns away.

Dear little one,
I see your soul pierced by the first man,
To claim an innocence as his own,
How could you have known.

Dear little one,
I see your fear, your confusion, your pain,
I see the world turning against you as a woman,
How could they have stolen your childhood.

Dear little one,
I see you drowning in everything,
The normal life, the rebel life, your life,
Did you have a choice in any one?

Dear little one,
I see you losing control,
It was the path they forced you on,
But the world makes you pay.

Dear little one,
I see your strength every day,
You woke up, you tried, you survived,
When the world didn't give you a reason to.

Dear little one,
I see you struggle with every task,
I want to tell you it will get better,
But I understand the peace of death.

Dear little one,
I want to release you from this fundamental thing,
It is not your fault, and never was.
Be at peace, little one.

Emotional pain

Emotional pain - what a term
To encompass the pains of trauma
My mind and body
Too distant and unfeeling
To face the truth

The purge of uncontrolled tears
As I drew the shadow of a protective stance
Over a young me
Something broke in my hardened spirit
To see that basic kindness
The pain of seeing for the first time
What had been missing from the beginning

The heavy tension at my heart
A confrontation I have refused to face
To know the paradox of control
To have it stolen
And then to willingly lose it to survive

The restlessness of the night
A seemingly fleeting craving to drown
Far from the surface where life exists
To understand the pain
Oh the pain - of simply breathing

A Breakthrough

How could I have only realised now
What it means to breathe without fear.
How could I have only realised now
That I have a place in this world.
How could I have only realised now
That every single thing I think, feel and do has meaning,
That not one of them should ever be dismissed,
That I by myself matter.
How could I have only realised now
That there are myriad beautiful aspects
To me - the way I see in others,
That even with, especially because of, the flaws, I'm perfect.

But how long will take for me to believe,
To truly believe in all these parts of me?
When will my soul sit back with my spirit,
And be at peace to commune together?

The Clouds

The solid white of the two shapes,
Against a backdrop of soft blue,
One leading boldly, the other yearning,
As they begin their journey across.

Her chest rises to the sun as her arms raise,
An arch in her back as she curves elegant,
Her eyes close as she settles into the seated dance,
A lazy confidence in herself and her destination.

She lowers her body to reach for her, just out of range,
Lifting her gaze for even a glimpse from near,
Her eyes cannot deny the yearning that's in her heart,
For just a taste of the life she boldly promises.

But as they move across they slowly start to wither,
Desperation claws up, reaching forward,
Urging them silently to merge, to keep their form,
Before this beautiful dream disappears completely.

But the journey across is unkind terrain,
Before long there's only a wisp of white,
To remind of what had been, of what could have been,
But only for those who had witnessed.

The sun continues to shine on the now-blank slate,
As if waiting to welcome another pair to start their journey,
I look around but the world is still,
The cool air drifts by as if taking a gentle inhale…

Then realisation hits - they're waiting for me to continue.

Forgiving myself

Have I placed my hope in my past,
Rather than my present or future?
Am I living in the past, and so
Disconnected in my present,
Absent in my future?

All this distress in the presence of my family,
Does my mind struggle to push them
To what I hope of a family?
All the fear of the voices that reside within,
Is there still the child struggling to be heard?

All the guilt and shame over the choices I've made,
Perhaps for survival, perhaps in ignorance,
Perhaps the only attempts I could conceive of
To break free, and perhaps for
Those short bursts of pleasure to numb the pain.

The past is set, they say,
With no hope of turning back,
Yet I long for something, anything, to be different,
Because it cannot be that this is it,
My past, my family, my life.

There is a truth I've missed - that though the past is set,
The present and future have yet to be written,
And I am the author of that story.
But the fear they continue to wield,
Keeps me from picking up the pen.

There is a subset to that truth,
Which the caged child within me
Needs to learn to believe,
That the door can be jarred open
And the adult me is building the muscle to do so.

Then there is the reality - that is perhaps as painful as the past,
That if I continue in this car of family neglect and pretense,
I will disappear from this world,
Because this family
Will not make space for the unabridged me.

Let me end on a hopeful note
To say that I choose life
And a place in this world,
If the past is set,
Then I want to create a future
Where there will be my own family, of love.

It hurts

It hurts to see
It hurts to dream of
It hurts to remember dreams of
A family loving, comforting, caring.

So much anger and hatred in those words and limbs
Hammering upon me again and again
To make sure I knew my place
Below and alone.

I see the judgement, disappointment, anger
In the eyes that rarely turned my way
Piercing through me to imprint their message
That I will never be enough.

A hurricane of conflicting feelings, never-ending
Of yearning, of blame, of pride, of criticism
Never grounding to protect, to comfort
Always surprised at the ache I reveal.

They bind together in the name of 'family'
Denying so vehemently that they mistake
Their pride in name as 'loyalty'
The blood we share as 'love'

I foolishly followed that tradition thinking it the only way
It was I who placed the rose-tinted glasses on all of us.
By giving up my control and my rightful anger
I added to the power they craved in the name - 'family'.

Then it was I who disappeared in their names for me.
They'd thrown the first shovels that covered me
But I allowed myself to be dug deeper and deeper in
All because of a child's dream of family, of love.

And when I could no longer stay buried for them
Had found the purity in strength to stand up and show myself
They scattered so quickly to hide behind 'respect'
That I was left shaking and unsteady, in their dust.

The Unformed Girl

Dread settles in the base of my gut,
My mind blanks, my face freezes in a forced smile,
Inside, every part of me stares in horror,
At the news of the impending birth of a girl.

One by one, they collapse with a scream -
Knowing the world will force her from the canal into the tight tube
of conformity,
Knowing her voice so clear at her first cry will be extinguished
soon,
Knowing I will have no power to change her fate for she lies in her
womb.

I run - away into the night, just away,
My spirit heaves dryly, unable to swallow the toxic fear,
My limbs are lead, chained in helplessness,
Before my mind can even think, my soul begins to mourn.

Wishes and dreams crowd in, overwhelming me,
'I wish I could do more for her, change more for her',
'I wish I could give more for her, more than I'm capable of',
'I wish she ceased to exist before she experiences the inevitable
pain'.

I force myself to stop, to ground myself in the present.
I immerse my mind with the warm glow that is my nephew,
I thought I'd already gotten my chance with him,
That with him I'd received my last hope.

My hope, my love, my chance,
A chance to start over with the clean slate of birth,
A chance to open my heart and see my love received wholly,
A chance to see my efforts to connect accepted always.

Could this be another chance, another hope?
Could this be another type of love I'd never dared to dream of?
One where I could give even more - more truth, more standing,
more heart -
For only I could open that first door for her.

Still a dream, still unformed, I remain conflicted.
I see now that my heart has barely opened,
To the unconditional love and trust a child can give,
And that by trying to push it shut, I've already taught her what I'd
feared.

Friday

The dawn is quiet, soft in its approach,
We sigh and plod forward, another day of work,
But there is a burgeoning excitement when it hits,
That today is the day before, the day of rest.

For me there is more, as it ignites my heart,
And love so full and pure flows freely as I recall
Wholesome moments from before, a precedent
For the moments we'll have today, the day we meet.

The anticipation carries me through the day of work,
Distracted by the glances to the protracted ticks of the clock,
My body weakened by the jitteriness of my stomach,
Finally ringing your doorbell, overwrought but grinning.

The high-pitched gibberish, the patter of tiny footsteps,
The eager calls of the name you christened me with,
Tugging the door, impatient to remove this barrier
To reveal, one bending the other lifting to greet.

The hours begin where nothing that week matters enough,
Where the instigators become bystanders in our play,
Where our eyes follow only the other and we're drawn
To move within our nucleus, where we can be with each other.

You look at me, and I respond with an indulgent smile,
You reach for me, and I bend to carry your weight,
Coming close, I instinctively lift to settle you on my lap,
To nuzzle and breathe you in, a balm to my soul.

Could it be that you will be the only man I love,
The only one I will remain in hell for, just for these moments.
The only one who loves me back, without reservation
Of the baggage bound to me, just for these moments.

A Rainy Day

Thoughts of the past barrage my mind,
Emotions flood in reaction, overwhelming my spirit,
I put my book away in defeat,
Surrendering to the onslaught against my inner peace.

But a glance towards the window distracts.
The darkening skies a foretoken of what's to come,
A quiet that has settled over the world outside,
A heaviness in the air tinged with the scent of rust.

As the first drops patter hesitantly, the winds sweep in,
The green wall of trees bend under its strength,
Pushed in whatever direction the gusts command,
But never breaking under its assault.

Thunder rumbles and the rain relinquishes its hold,
The sheets fall, bowing the branches further,
They merge to form an impenetrable wall outside,
Its deafening cascade silencing everything inside.

It sinks inward, a shield against the inner storm,
Relieved I turn into comfort, cocooned by nature,
Watching serenely as it pours its abundance,
And disperses the gloom gathered during the day.

As the skies empty their burdens,
Light peeks through the fading clouds,
They drift leisurely to reveal their caster -
The moon, its fullness holding a quiet power,
A beacon for wandering souls.

Sunrise

Barely a moment's rest last night,
My head weighs heavily as the alarm rings,
I look around blearily as the curtains slide open,
And blink, surprised to see the sun cheekily peeking back.

It edges just around the clean white buildings,
Its emerging glow spilling richly across the green,
Light strokes of yellow and orange painted liberally across the sky,
Its generous warmth pulsing swiftly towards me.

Its energy ignites my spirit and my tiredness clears away,
My body stretches luxuriously under the sun's radiance,
Any tightness eased away, no remnant pain left behind,
I smile, unbelievably grateful, my vision blurring with tears.

For it was not too long ago when my entire being was stifled,
The agony of living with the past permeated throughout,
To know I breathe freely now, no longer tormented,
Liberates my heart, which lifts to herald the day ahead.

Thirty

Thirty – A ceremonious stop in this long path,
Where people were waiting expectantly for your arrival,
To continue the story of your life from the last stop,
To show them the trophies you've gathered along the way.

Thirty – Another stop in this long path,
An opportunity for you to catch your breath, refuel,
To stand still for just a moment to look back on that path,
And search within yourself for what you've done thus far.

Thirty – Another night in this long path,
When the stars scatter wide across the sky's expanse,
Where you sit alone in this vast universe,
Still unsure of your place, but with myriad steps to take next.

Thirty – The time and place to stop in this long path,
To drop the baggage you've been burdened with on your journey,
To turn away from those who had joined uninvited,
And gaze upon the other paths carved, and wonder.

Thirty – An unexpected stop in this long path,
A decision made long ago to never arrive here,
To unburden the self and the world of your path,
But still having fought to hope to give yourself a chance.

Thirty – A stop to celebrate in this long path,
For you have made space for your life amongst others,
For you have a past to look back on, dreams of a future to move
towards,
For you, and only you, could have made this life and can change
this life.

ACT II: ANGER

"By disowning our traumatized parts..., by disconnecting from them emotionally or losing consciousness of them via dissociation, we preserve our hearts and souls from growing as bitter as our circumstances. We hold out hope for the future and we keep going."

- Janina Fisher, Healing the Fragmented Selves of Trauma Survivors

The Day After A Break

My spirit tosses restlessly,
I sense its disturbance and prod gently,
It lashes out with pain,
Withdrawing to cocoon as tears stream silently.

My heart cannot find the calm it had just before,
My body sinks heavy with tension,
My eyes struggle to stay open in midday -
My spirit drags me under to show me.

I am brought back to the greetings of delight.
I knew they had remained only in words,
For my experiences had not been welcomed,
And so I had stayed silent, to observe.

With uncanny consistency, each snatched the spotlight back,
When their experiences appeared even slightly faded,
When their opinions were a degree different,
When they needed just a bit more to feel like more.

Annoyance was hedged out by repulsion,
As her snide missiles sought out vulnerable spots to unbalance me,
And when she took pleasure in her children's failures,
I was simply baffled that the irony had escaped her.

But it was the treatment of the young child that shattered me,
An unnecessary repeat performance by poor understudies
Of constant vitriol and dismissal that cut deep into his heart
And mind, as his tiny hands reached for mine instead to wipe his
tears.

Indignation fires, flames licking hot and white,
How dare they pray with one hand and slap with the other,
How dare they preach for the suffering in the world, turning from
their children's.

But the blaze burns out just as quickly - useless, this is just useless.

A voice whispers back - "No, sometimes anger for me is enough".

Intergenerational Trauma

As I expand, I look within, coaxing her to reveal more of herself
She continues to tear, draining a bottomless pit of hope
Anger and understanding war as I fling the dusty curtain wide open
To expose the rotten branches they've covered for generations.

The guise of parental pride -
Put forth as separate from personal stake,
But simply a carrot on a stick they fashioned with their dreams,
Forever dangling and never accomplished.

The twist of parental love -
A ploy they began which will never end,
To extract love for unmet needs while yours they cast aside,
Ending only in a warped tangle no one can win.

The mask of parental discipline -
A gavel wielded for glory and name,
It herds with insidious shadows that threaten,
Power distorting all morality and reason.

The irony of parental acceptance -
Where birth is intentioned to start anew,
Yet it is anger that rips through when their mould is theirs,
The shame of association to this incomplete set.

A vicious cycle that refuses to be broken,
I urge her, gently, to separate and walk away,
For within us is a clarity they adamantly remain blind to,
That shows us that their foundation, does not have to be ours.

The Hell They Created

They taught me to be afraid,
To fear being one who felt free and happy, for that could only
mean trouble,
To fear the choices that would free you, and keep glued to the
comfort of misery,
To fear standing up for justice true and right, for self-preservation.

They taught me to nurture the toxicity within,
To view with suspicious eyes and heart,
To dole out prejudice to strangers, pit family against each other,
Every difference a flaw to be flambèed for perverse pleasure.

They taught me to love conditionally,
To gift love when your terms are met,
To speak with love when they act to your liking,
That by law and blood a connection can be termed as 'love', to use
against.

They taught me to be small,
They pushed forward their narrative, when I tried to find my voice,
They diminished my narrative, when I did manage to speak,
And buried it completely, before anyone could see the true me.

I withdrew, and they ran quickly in relief,
I refused, and they took offense,
I stopped trying, and they took it for acceptance,
I remained affable, and their minds happily forgot mine to reset
their narrative.

Why am I still here in this hell that will never change,
For innocent children who face the inevitable?
For a family who will always choose to see me as they want?
To sit in their picture of perfection, never revealing the ugliness
within?
Why am I continuing to play for their narrative?

Shelter

Shelter – a safe place,
To protect from the demons that come hunting,
To provide for what you lack in your hour of need,
To shield from the reality you cannot face.

To live her childhood without a shelter to begin
And then come of age, ripened for predation,
When their shadowy tendrils seized in rapacious glory,
Was to know naked unbearable terror.

The ceaseless assault on the mind and body
Spread the cracks on an exhausted spirit
And just one more was enough to split her completely,
To escape to the shelter she'd created within.

Then to discover that she had none to begin with
Was because it was her who was their unwitting shelter,
For unable to face their lack, they failed to witness the demons they
bore
Who, confined to the darkness of their home, sought out the only
one they could -

The youngest, her core of generosity and openness
A seductive light to those with darkness within,
For without having been taught of a voice, she knew not of one to
speak
Of the depravedness they tormented her with.

Shelter - *your* safe place - was a *person* you desecrated,
The tortured soul she's only just beginning to soothe.
Just wait for her wings to gather the strength to lift off,
For then her voice will soar, never to be silenced by you again.

Two and a Half Years Old

The crack comes down with the slash of their shout.
His face drops and his shoulders hunch,
His bottom lip quivers, pushing forward,
His eyes widen as they fill with tears.

He moves to me as my hands reach for him,
One around his shoulders in instinctive protection,
The other rubs his chest gently to soothe.
I pray his brimming tears don't spill over.

Seeing our reactions they respond quickly to brush away.
They too reach, but to point to his overreaction,
Then to demand he seek comfort from their arms.
He turns to me instead, to bury himself in mine.

My arms envelope him to shield from this world,
I whisper promises of safety and love in our embrace,
More truth than white lies to pacify,
As my heart staggers with pain for him.

For no child should have to turn away to cry,
No child should have to seek comfort from others,
No child should have to bear such fear,
All because of the pride and arrogance of parents.

The Family Portrait

Here we sit in different corners,
The two with pride in their eyes as they take stock,
The two with alternating blank and frustrated looks,
And us two cuddled close, gazing adoringly at each other.

I laugh secretly to think of another chancing upon this moment,
A quick flash the only tell of a picture stolen,
And the disparity between this and theirs,
Are what tell the uncensored story of this family.

My mind flips through the numerous photos taken,
Faces set neutrally, eyes blank of emotion,
Bodies positioned in apparent intimacy – though,
The subtle tension of limbs kept slightly apart betray.

As I continue to shrewdly scan across,
The dipping in his face catches me by surprise.
I slow down and study the gradual decline,
From the amused light in his young eyes, to the angry scowl.

Disconcerted, I focus on narrowing it down,
To the point in time when his demeanour had tipped over,
But the lengthening period between each portrait,
Throws me off this duty, back to the present.

I sit back and reflect on a journey not spoken of,
Which an album had unknowingly captured -
One where my expression never changed,
But the stagnated collection reveals.

To The Spirits Within

To my 'fight' spirit,
I thank you for standing up for my justice,
For trying to find a way to rationalise the trauma dealt,
Struggling constantly to validate our existence.

To my 'flight' spirit,
I thank you for withdrawing from such misery,
For numbing me to the constant terror and pain,
So I could get through the nightmares, to wake up every day.

To my 'freeze' spirit,
I thank you for keeping me alive,
For without having played dead at the predators worst,
My body would most certainly have been buried by now.

To my 'submit' spirit,
I thank you for helping me survive through the worst,
That even through my conflicted feelings toward you,
You never stop looking out for me when they come hunting.

To the predators who invaded my mind and body,
You will never be thanked or welcomed,
Instead you will meet the army within me,
Stronger than anything you will ever fire.

To the 'harsh critic', the parents poison,
You are my greatest disappointment,
For instead of love, you fed me the toxicity of blame and guilt,
And doomed a part of me to forever fight against myself.

To my 'attach' spirit, my inner child,
I thank you for surviving through it all, dear little one,
That despite everything they did to you,
You still believe so pure and true of a future for us.

To my 'rational' spirit, my beloved adult,
I thank you for all the work you've put in for us,
To speak to and understand every spirit,
So that we may all find the calm we need, to thrive.

The Woman Within

I close my eyes and breathe deeply,
A pulsing begins deep within me, stronger with every beat,
A rush of energy surges up and my eyes open, with a grin –
She has emerged.

My senses are heightened as I feel her settle into the body,
I'm drawn to her movements, assured as she is in them,
She feels me hesitate at the cusp and brushes against me invitingly,
Wanting, I take the step aside to welcome.

She lifts herself confidently as she sweeps in,
I wonder why she had been called upon to save,
Knowing my fear to embrace, she moves to possess,
And I drift, losing my grasp.

Unlike before, she wanders while she waits,
It had been this weakness in facing the dark reality,
One of many moments before (we cannot recall which),
That had birthed her into existence.

She crosses a mirror and stops to survey,
So alike in looks yet so different in demeanour,
Knowing I yearn for hers she holds it out of reach,
So only together, we could continue to survive.

When she senses the sea of emotions have calmed within me,
Feels my mind restlessly knocking against,
She curtsies and withdraws gracefully.
And I wake up, alone, still wanting.

Who Do You Want To Be?

I thought I wanted to be who you wanted me to be -
The daughter who connected when the other didn't,
The friend who cared much more than anyone else,
The mediator and protector you needed.

But that's all you, isn't it.
I have given so much of myself just for you,
I gained satisfaction only at your acceptance
Until I failed to be what you wanted me to be, for you.

Setting out to find what only I could want
Has created such turmoil for all of us,
Without my submission and yearning in this mix,
The cold, hard emptiness stands out starkly.

You wielded the weapons you knew would work,
Loyalty to you, responsibility for the innocent,
Engulfing the burdens to guilt and confuse
So I would stay on that thin line, never to tip over.

You have only seen my strengths for your use,
For far too long. Exploiting a need for love and approval,
Puppeting knowledge and perception deemed acceptable,
I see now that I have always been your sacrificial lamb - celebrated
only as,
An offering.

With the willpower I've forged in the fire of trauma,
I rise and shatter the twisted altar you'd chained me to,
I take everything I am for myself and those I choose
And relieved, surge ahead into the life I desire.

Making My Choice

Tears sting my eyes as I wade through the mucky past,
Trophies gathered stand along the way, dusty and unused,
They had cost my efforts, more than was needed,
For they were won in an attempt to finally earn your pride.

The child within me yearned far too much for it,
And I hadn't realised then that could never have come to pass,
So I needlessly grinded on the well-worn path of accolades,
Ignoring the dread in my heart and the silent cries of my spirit.

I try to pinpoint when exactly that fire had sparked in me -
Was it the first time I purged the pain from within
And realised I could use those words to sketch my story?
Or was it the first time I realised what had been missing from the
beginning?

The cathartic release of my breath was a revelation,
To know that I had held thoughts of fading away,
By holding my fears so tightly as you had encouraged,
Thereby holding even the gift of freely breathing, hidden from
myself.

It has been an avalanche of release from then on,
Shoving out everything you'd flooded into my space,
Finally turning toward the voices to challenge,
And that secret smile that tugged when I got to say for the first
time NO.

Sloughing off these choices that were never truly my own,
I finally peer through the cracks of the clearing grime,
And understand that to kindle the wakening power within,
I must voice again and again, that this is my life.

The Drive Home

He inches forward,
Nudging my foot,
A hungry guinea pig
Is hard to ignore.
But I cannot seem to take that step,
To give him what he needs,
For I myself was expectant
And left shaken.

The loud upbeat music,
A contrast to the tension,
Hanging heavily
Within the four doors.
His forgetfulness of a well-known route
As anger simmered,
Her subtle gesture of a hand extended
To caution.

An unexpected reveal,
In reality long overdue,
My choices a signal
Of the bigger truth within.
But they remain blind,
Ignoring my previous laments,
And repeat mindlessly
What they were taught.

My previous coaching
For this very moment
When simple statements
Should have sufficed
Are tossed out
When my inner child senses
Apprehension
And blurts out my accomplishments.

Stubbornly unmoved
He touts the age-old mantra
Of glory and name
With every piece of paper earned
Oblivious to my growing grief
For my inner child
As she cowers
Struck back by his obvious shame.

There is only one seat
In this journey forward,
But somehow their deprecation
Cannot be thrown off.
I sit here unsettled,
Lost as to how to guide us onward,
And hopelessness sneaks up,
Its chains clinking menacingly.

A Dinner Invitation

A friendly invite extended,
The apple offered from the disguised witch,
Luscious sweet relief a promise,
Sickness deep within the reality.

I know better now than before
To see you as you are
Not how I have yearned for you to be
And so I know what your play will be.

Holding your cards close to lure,
Waiting for my guard to fade to reveal mine,
Pushing my chips in confident of my place,
Slamming your cards down to empty me.

Now why would I do to myself
What I have done countless times before,
If there was ever the chance to learn
It would be now, with the strength I've gained.

I cannot go back to what was before
Where I'm stifled in the guilt you wrap me in,
Not when I've seen where my life can go
Where I've raced swiftly ahead in my dreams.

Seeking

A listening year, always welcoming of my story,
Knowledge given, to ease and strengthen my mind,
Methods taught, to ground my spirit in the present,
Understanding perfectly, the pain my body conveys.

A perspective given, so different to what I've known,
Because of those who tortured, and twisted views,
To say instead there was strength, and resilience,
Where I'd simply seen surviving, barely.

Another given, of the ability to choose,
To learn it was possible, to voice my choices,
Breathed life into my body, lifting it up,
And power surged into my spirit, at long last.

Moving them out of my space, protecting it fiercely,
Shedding the choices forced upon, breathing freely,
Averting love once given unreservedly, now to only the few,
Liberating the spirit they chained, for themselves.

Now they fear, for what will become of them,
When there is none to placate, their hurt pride,
None to steady and steer, through their dysfunction,
None to love despite, their selfish manipulation.

My story will continue, without them I hope,
I will laugh with abandon, unafraid and trying,
I will close my eyes, unguarded and trusting,
I will finally stand still, on the solid ground I build.

Repeat It

Throw, throw, throw,
Throw away the gifts that remind,
Throw away the habits that hold back,
Throw away the choices that weren't mine.

Wait, wait, wait,
Wait for the fear of relapse,
Wait for the fear of accusations,
Wait for the fear of an untrodden path ahead.

Move, move, move,
Move, harried by the unrelenting expectations,
Move, disturbed by the constant reminders,
Move, just shut down to survive.

Stop, stop, stop,
Stop, and reach for those helping hands,
Stop, and learn how to stand on your own,
Stop, and celebrate how far you've come.

Be, be, be,
Be steady as you stride forward,
Be calm as you observe within,
Just be, for you deserve this space.

ACT III: SADNESS

"It takes real courage to look squarely at trauma and addiction and let yourself see what's really going on. It may feel too hard to admit [the truth]... . Everything in you may want to fight the truth, may tell you it's too much or too scary, or the flip side, may dismiss it as unimportant. All of these are ways your mind shuts down to protect you from too much truth. You can honor and respect that this helped you survive."

- Lisa M. Najavits, Finding Your Best Self: Recovery from Addiction, Trauma, or Both

Cravings

It's a silent push from within,
A natural urge to quench,
An emptiness to be filled,
A hunger to satisfied.

Ironically the void roots from an overwhelming,
Too many demanding for the steady one,
The perfect one, the forgiving one, the kind one,
Too many demanding for the person they need.

The questions never stop coming,
The pressure presses around me,
My senses heighten in response,
Looking wildly for any escape.

My mind descends into a fogged state,
A natural protection against a hyper system,
A system that can no longer cope with the burden,
Of being what everyone needs.

It's somewhere in the back of my mind,
That I should resist these urges,
There's a list I think,
What was it?

I'm brought back to that first state,
Its fumes seductively slipping in,
The somehow sweet yet tart tang,
The glorious ignite to my senses.

Oh how everything disappears,
It's like nothing matters anymore but the next sip,
Each one surging through me,
Pushing me higher and higher.

And there's that moment of absolute bliss,
After that one drink that pushes you to the top,
Where you're soaring way above and beyond,
Reality so miniscule and far below - barely aware of it.

I don't want to go on,
And tell you what happens when I tip over,
I'm remembering that list now,
Sigh.

It's a crash you're not even aware of at first -
Who can stop the next drink when you've hit that high,
But it pushes you over, tumbling, into darkness,
And when you come to, you're flat on your face.

It's not just the pounding in your brain,
And your stomach pitching unsteadily,
It's the slap reality awakens you with,
And the piercing pain that threatens to tear you apart from within.

The only way to stop it, you think, is to drink again,
Till your body is absolutely numb to all of it,
And you can never stop for fear of that crash,
It'll rule your very life as it burns it to the ground.

A hundred and nine days - please fight back,
Don't believe the lies it whispers,
You are so much more than your pain,
You are so much stronger than you know.

Stop Talking About 'Hitler'

I see you've started your fishing expedition,
Seemingly off-hand remarks of justice,
Tailored just to entice me in to converse -
Anger sparks and breaks through my fog.

I'm about to retort with righteousness,
When my mind curiously questions.
Stunned, I hold my anger back
And retreat inward to contemplate.

Did you make the connection
Between the injustice in the world
And the sickness that lived in your home.
Do you know of my anger?

Did you see too the roots of shame and hurt,
The guilt you've tangled in between
Where my anger has sprouted from.
Do you know what you caused?

But then you turn away,
Your disappointment sweeping across,
Piercing my heart once again,
To think that you could remain so blind.

Memories

I had hoped I would be writing another list
Of more achievements in another month of sobriety.
But looking back over these weeks,
I think I have fallen back.

I wish that it would be true
That when I was certain these bridges were burnt
That the memories of the hurt they caused
Would have died with that knowledge.
Because with every step forward, and back,
I was reminded of a past I cannot erase.
The pain swept in, choking my very breath,
And I craved so desperately to numb myself.

It was arrogance that called me 'lazy'
For having chosen to numb over fighting through the pain.
An arrogance born out of pride for resisting temptation,
But an arrogance nonetheless that hurt a part of me.
For how can I blame the past me for succumbing
When I myself have said to those I love
That if there was any way I could take away their pain
I would do so in a heartbeat.

But I continue to fight this battle,
One I was thrust into without choice.
Little respite I get as they advance again,
Forcing me to remember, with fresh wounds.
I find the strength in me to stand my ground,
Cheering my exhausted spirit with stale phrases
And the truth - one day we will make new memories,
Ones that can only bring joy, never pain.

A Surprise Bouquet

I awaken to the sounds of my neighbour,
A day to catch up on the tasks of the week for her,
A day to catch up on rest for me
But this time even ten hours of sleep is too little.

I turn into the welcoming softness of my pillow
And ignore the buzz from my door, playing dead,
But the insistent knocks annoy enough to get me up
Marching with a scowl, ready to bark at the intruder.

The view of the cheery colours knock out all irritation.
I stare in shock at the bouquet, and the stranger holding it.
She announces it is for me, handing it over,
With my mind blank, I accept it shakily.

I turn into my home as the door closes behind me,
Searching for a card, unwilling to believe.
I see the familiar scrawl and it dawns,
Unable now to believe of such a friendship.

I am touched as I read of praise and admiration,
I am touched by her efforts to honour it as such,
I am touched by a love that reaches across oceans,
I am touched to be thought of at all.

I am reminded that this is a battle spanning years,
And that my struggles may take as long to subside,
That the triggers will keep attacking causing despair,
Which I will never overcome if I sink helpless in acceptance.

And as much as my birth family deliberately withhold
In their attempts to manipulate me back into their lair,
My found family has overwhelmingly and wholly given
To nurture and uplift me to the person they know I can be.

A Step In

I hear the critic's voice as theirs.
I pluck up the courage to lift my head
To look at their shame in the eye,
And see my own face looking back at me.
To feel that gut punch of failure,
I almost give in to the temptation to withdraw.
But I try to find the courage to take the step
To admit that I've lost control and need help
And my mind, so conditioned by their fear,
Refusing to expose, refusing to accept,
Begins to fog in retaliation.
My defenses spit back.

The battle is brutal.
Battered inside and out
By the war I have waged
On the pathways they set.
But something begins to glow,
Just a flicker that spreads warmth,
And though I am covered in wounds,
I notice the one healing.
Yet it doesn't end the fight but starts anew.
Again and again I am called upon to stand,
To poke and prod, to question and think,
And mercilessly break the walls carefully built.
My feelings flood unrestrained,
With every event unrelated I see my pain,
Intensifying to a climax of utter sadness,
Forcing me to my knees, as I break down and weep.
And it is right then that my spirit begs me to accept
That this journey is one only I have chosen,
That by holding on to hope that they would too,
I had dragged us into a pit of despair.

I sigh, starting the fight again.
I had failed again, but vow to do better,
Grasping the bottom rung of the worn ladder,
To lift us back out again -
I am shocked to feel strength in my body,
Shocked when I look down to see only scars,
Shocked at the ease at which I lift my head back up,
Shocked at how quick the corner of my lips lift -
And joy washes through me.
For though I am just beginning,
I am certain now that I deserve more,
And it remains to be seen just how much.

Drip, drip, drip

Prat-tat-tat – squeak!
I'm jolted out of a restless sleep,
My eyes shoot open as my ears prick up,
But from the neck down, I am frozen.

Prat-tat-tat – slowing,
My heart is racing, thumping loudly,
But as it plays in time with the unknown,
Just my forehead wrinkles in confusion.

Prat-tat-tat – slowing,
My eyes grow accustomed to the dark,
Searching, my mind catches up to reason,
I must still be alone in my space.

Tat-tat-tat – steady,
I become aware of the tension in my body,
Slowly I test its movement, slightly raising,
And then peel my sweaty limbs off the cool bed.

Tat-tat-tat – steady,
Even with reason, fear allows only a cautious inch forward,
I glance to the left, hoping my guinea pigs had hidden,
Relief floods for the prey instinct that protects them.

Tat-tat-tat – steady,
A sweep of the unoccupied area offers solace to my mind,
A calm drifts inward, slowing my system,
I am safe, there is no one in my space.

Tat-tat-tat – steady,
Curiosity pipes up now, looking for the unknown,
Almost slipping, I feel around to switch on the light,
And laugh incredulously at the simple leak revealed.

Drip-drip-drip – steady,
A bucket to collect, a towel to dampen the sound,
My hand reaches absently for the phone to call,
And recoils to clutch my chest where fear has gathered again.

Drip-drip-drip – steady,
What sense would it make to call them in distress,
The very ones I'd been terrified had invaded again,
Here I am safe, just me alone in my space.

Drip-drip-drip – steady,
I look at my guinea pigs poking their heads out,
Looking to me to protect and keep them safe,
It grounds me enough to push back against the fear.

Drip-drip-drip – slowing,
Reason knocks gently and I smile in gratitude,
Switching off the supply, the slowing drops echo within me,
A chant I repeat that I will keep this door firmly shut.

Drip-drip – slowing,
But there is pain, such deep pain,
To know that I must make such a choice,
To be alone, to be safe.

Drip – slowing,
And anger sparks from that pain,
Trying to make some sense of a choice they made,
To turn away from me.

I watch the last drops descend as if in slow motion,
A reflection of the last remnants of pain receding,
My mind and body will always summon it first to protect,
But how I choose to continue to protect will be up to me.

Garden Home

I pointed out the wriggling centipede,
Unearthed by the rudeness of rain,
Joined by its siblings in their course,
To track back to their home deep within.

Then I showed you the curled millipede,
Alone and vulnerable out on the pathway,
Instinctually shielding the only way it knew how,
Just a stop before it can head to its safety.

We picked the green fruits of the land,
Still unripe but ready soon to yield,
I told you of the seed hidden within,
Which would bear more for the land if planted.

You exclaimed in delight and amazement,
You bent to observe closer without interfering,
You tilted your head as you listened and learned,
And yet I made the adult mistake of not believing.

But then you pointed your finger at the arthropods,
And proclaimed they were heading home 'to sleep',
You plucked the budding berries, laid them on the ground,
And declared 'home' when asked.

It is grateful I am that you accept without question,
That 'home' is a place for refuge and nourishment,
While I look on with a ridiculous pity for myself,
That I struggle to offer something I never had.

The Old Path

I watch you beaming for me,
And observe the shadows that pass over your face,
I watch you grip your shell,
Weighing on you as the night goes on,
I watch you slowly withdraw,
Struggling to hold on till our date ends.

My heart aches as I watch,
Seeming to nudge me to do more,
But just as I reach forward
My mind clicks in
And all those old pathways
Light up to confuse.

I hear her voice,
A hint of hysteria but confidently loud,
Telling me I shouldn't interfere in case of trouble.
I hear his voice,
Snapping out, not bothering to hide its irritation,
Telling me not to be distracted by others.

When I'm jolted back,
I freeze.
My eyes dart from side to side
Wondering who to follow –
Their teachings which sound so cold,
Or the voice within, warm but hushed.

I stay glued to the spot
Not daring to make the choice,
So you stand afar too in your own pain.
I see you trying to inch forward
And your strength spurs me
To look back and question.

I think of nature – flora and fauna,
Of my deep love to nurture,
And then the mixed signals she gave,
Equally convinced I could not be responsible
And proud that I take on after her,
All the while pushing to keep more trouble out.

When I resisted and welcomed them,
She was there always –
To tell me I was doing it all wrong,
To shove me aside and take over,
Never teaching me how to instead,
Then sulking when she did it all alone.

I remember too his sermons,
Coming on the backs of those parables,
Teaching of empathy, even praying for all,
But when I acted accordingly
His fury blasted at me to hold back, to turn away,
To take care first of one's own self.

It was impossible to reason with him
As he stood across a chasm I could never reach,
Angry when I defied more and more,
Just so he could hear me all the way over,
Blind when I submissively followed,
Just for one thing he could be proud of.

All these old pathways can never show how,
To take on challenges confident in your abilities,
To teach with kindness and nurture,
To empathise and love all regardless,
To stand close to touch each other's lives,
To never need more than your self to be enough.

Forgive me, my dear friend,
For holding back, for thinking it was right,
I am resetting pathways long set
By the terror and longing of a child,
But I swear I will overcome them
And learn the right way to love you.

The Happy

We grow up hearing it again and again,
To think of others who have it worse,
To think that this is minor,
Inconsequential in the bigger scheme of things,
So suddenly what was once big in our lives,
Diminishes to nothing more than a speck.

We're told not to waste,
Not because of the principle on its own
But because of famine and drought elsewhere,
Such gargantuan concepts,
They pay little head to its complexity,
Focusing instead on taming us.

They speak of the politics of the world,
That ridiculous subject where any opinion ventured
Raises them to a status of importance,
But they fail to make room in the conversations
For the everyday deeds of ordinary us,
The very deeds they forget are the bedrock of politics.

So when we have our everyday triumphs,
How could they mean anything more -
They remind us of those full names with prestige,
That we are nowhere there and so cannot be seen.
Our young rebellious hearts, full of anger and ambition,
Say silently, "Just wait and see".

But success takes myriad steps
Both forwards and backwards
And if every step is belittled
Then how can they recognise
When we've reached that step,
The step that earns us a full name with prestige.

By then we are much too old to acknowledge
The promises our young selves have made,
And so after we have rocketed to absolute euphoria,
We crash into a state of such devastation,
Unable to understand why we cannot stay on that high,
Unable to remember why we so badly needed to see their pride.

Let's not forget how they inserted us
Into this infinite loop
So we can find a way to break free
Of this dysfunctional cycle
Acknowledging all parts - sad and joyful -
To finally stay grounded in the happy.

Dawn

I used to treasure twilight,
That time when the mad and the sad are up
Haunted by their own demons
Trying to escape but somehow seeking them.
It was the absolute silence I craved,
When my space would be finally cleared of them
And though their voices would then appear
I could drown them out in peace.
Because when the sun rose,
So too would my monsters
And I was no longer alone,
No longer safe in my silent bubble.

It's with sadness that I look back on that time,
To realise that I too never escaped my demons,
Doggedly pursued all day and night in body and mind,
Imprisoned to perform the rituals they demanded.
Living with such terror and despair,
Never safe, always on alert,
Who wouldn't seek desperately
The comfort of the night,
For in that inky blankness one can hide and disappear,
Cushioned by the silence that protects against the horrors,
But still look up and away from a life of never-ending pain
And see hope twinkling, just out of reach.

I'm grateful to the past me who found that courage
To take the first terrifying step out of that prison,
Even if it was in the dead of the night
When they were sound asleep in their warm beds.
And then the strength it took to keep out of it,
Fighting against a lifetime within it,
Their voices so convincing that I deserve just that,
Aided by their constant whips and lashes on the outside.
Strangely, it was the sadness that saved me,
When every part within me chorused in unison
With pleading moans that pierced through the fog,
And my eyes finally cleared to see the true extent of the wounds inflicted.

It was like I had shed the dusk;
No longer haunted, I didn't need to stay up
To keep the demons company
And I slept deeply, finding silence in my dreams.
Awakening refreshed, though still dark;
I sit and wait unafraid
Watching the sky lightening at the corner
Before the sun itself appears in all its glory.
It is a heavenly sight to see the day arriving,
For the hope once so far away, now lives within me,
And as the light dawns, my heart lifts unburdened,
Knowing now I have the power to keep myself safe.

A Dream

I cannot take my eyes off
The gun in her hand
Its beady eye solely focused
On the life before it
The life that is mine.

She waves me forward
Each a whip lash
Till I reach the edge
And stare down
The dizzying height.

I am torn between the two
Both violent ends
But one a step I can take
The other with no choice
So I make my move.

But when my body turns
Her hand lowers
I look at her confused
Her face a mirror
And she asks how.

I say this isn't my first
I've stood here before
With a gun I held
Sobbing to myself
To make the choice.

There's a moment of silence
And then she whispers
That she thought
There was only one.
With pain in my heart, I say,

"Staying alive is a choice,
You may never find peace,
But you will find hope,
Dead, you will find peace,
But there will never be hope.

I realise now I always had hope,
Even through the darkest times,
It was a naïve, childish hope,
But it was hope enough,
To keep surviving.

But if you have none,
Death is a relief,
Finally an end to suffering,
Finally an end to pain,
And finally peace for your soul.

What will you choose,
When the time comes,
Which path do you see,
When you look ahead,
Where will you go."

What Will I Tell You When You Grow Up?

I feel the lightness in my heart,
That terrible tension lifted from it,
As my mind finally arrives at this conclusion,
The only one that can keep me safe,
And I close my eyes in relief,
For though I'd made all the decisions prior,
I see now they were tests for them and me,
On how far we could go before the inevitable,
A truth I knew from the beginning,
But the desperate hope of a child refused to accept.

With this certainty my mind looks ahead,
Down this new path I've chosen to embark on,
And a delirious giggle escapes my lips –
The options! The freedom! The joy!
I am absolutely flabbergasted,
At what had been kept from me all these years.
There'd always been a shadowed veil over this path,
Unrelentingly guarded by them out of their fear,
Ruthlessly shooting insults and punishment from its door,
To ensure I too would learn to fear it.

I am thankful for the strength it took to challenge,
Learning of the fear instead of accepting,
Trying to edge forward instead of stagnating,
Facing my shame instead of defending,
To come to this point of moving beyond them.
But while I rejoice for myself, I weep too,
For one of the walls broken was around my heart,
And as I look back at what I've left behind,
My heart is pierced by the pain I see on their faces,
Absolutely wrenched that you are now beyond me.

I am forced to remind myself again and again,
Of the warped path they had put me on,
In contrast to the lone but freeing path,
Which only serves to highlight to me,
The path I've left you on.
I'm racked with guilt and shame,
Constantly turning toward the path behind,
Wondering if I should have done more,
Reminding myself, again, that I've done all I could,
That the only way to truly live is to move forward.

So I settle for the little bits I get to have with you,
The one spot of warmth and love from the before,
And the glimpses of another path I show you,
For you to always know of a better way,
To live, to love, to reach for, to dream of,
Where I'll be waiting for you no matter what.
Though I wonder what I can say on the fateful day,
When you finally look back and forth and ask
Of my story – the reason I had to leave,
Of why I had no choice but to leave you behind.

The Full Story

I don't want to think of what they went through,
But as I read the story of an immigrant family,
I can't help but wonder about mine,
What is my unabridged story?

I think of the bits they've told me,
Trying to piece them together,
To see the picture they bring to life,
But those missing form too large a hole.

More than that, much more,
Is the lens with which I view half the picture,
The hurt I cannot put away even for this,
For their betrayal is too large to bear.

As I slowly move from anger,
I ease into sadness, as intense but more open,
And so I pick up the unfinished picture,
Wondering if just this could explain it all for me.

I think of that story from the son of immigrants,
Ignoring, dismissing, blaming – were they the same?
Could his parents have neglected him as mine did,
Would his parents have crossed the line as mine did.

Is it the lens or is it them, I can't tell,
What is standing in the way of us crossing over,
To learn of the others' vulnerabilities and shame,
To forgive the betrayals done to the other.

I feel a qualifying, concluding statement is needed,
To say that betraying their dreams of the perfect family,
Is nothing compared to betraying their child of a safe home.
The line is crossed, the picture remains unfinished.

Released

Saturdays allow laziness to be termed relaxation,
So I stretch out and bask in the measly sunlight,
Streaming through heavy clouds into my windows,
Eyes following those who insist on working,
Unable to put aside an ethic drilled in,
And wonder if I should drift into a second nap.

It's then that my mind decides to ask,
Coyly, gently nudging me,
If I'd noticed it was the first time,
That my heart was as relaxed as my body,
My spirit as lazily stretched out as my limbs,
My soul steady with an undisturbed peace.

I sit up slightly, sleep cleared, and think,
A quick search reveals nothing lurking,
So I dig deeper, reaching in to tug,
At the intense emotions that were a part of me,
In an utterly abused life,
But they simply sigh and turn over, finally resting.

My mind goes back to just a few days ago,
Knowing it could not be failure if I was trying again,
This time armed with compassion for myself,
Slowly stepping out, grounding throughout,
Focusing on the joy of rising with the sun,
A smile to thank my spirit for its tenacity.

I wonder curiously why my newfound knowledge,
Doesn't trigger my resting emotions as usual,
Could realising my anger for the world,
Was mere disappointment in their ignorance,
Enough to soothe and settle it finally,
The last domino after guilt, shame, sadness?

Or was it the confirmation of my inner child's cries,
That even then she was absolutely right -
To dream of a saviour, a different family,
When every adult in her life had failed her,
And a child had been imprisoned in a war zone -
For that was actually the law of the land.

So it was just the vindication I needed,
To release me of any remnant guilt I had left,
From my actions of teasing out the entanglements,
And finally pushing away from their toxicity,
Absolving myself of all the blame they placed,
On a young child they themselves had abused.

And knowing, oh knowing,
That I owe nothing to those who did that to me,
For I deserve to feel safe and at peace,
Nurtured, supported, nourished, loved,
All the things I can now give to myself,
In this beautiful space I have created for myself.

Future?

Is it okay to give up on what I thought my future would be,
Having been promised to be the most fulfilling out of all?

Is it okay to be happy for those who pursue that future,
Knowing it was a dream of my past though never in my future?

Is it okay to cry tears of joy when they have that future,
Mixed in with a sadness that doesn't penetrate deeply?

Is it okay to imagine how this dream would have been,
While I spend happy moments with your future?

Is it okay to let go of the anger for those who keep this future for
me,
When they are the reason I have given it up?

Is it okay to move on to a future I can't imagine,
Simply because today is a day I never imagined?

AFTERWORD

You may be asking now if I've got my land legs?

It's a long road when it comes to recovery from trauma and I'm just starting. But having established my safe space - be it the physical space that I'm assured now is just mine and the good people in my life who I'm doing my best to trust - I do feel much steadier. More than just surviving, I want to thrive in *my* life (yes, my therapist was right). And so, poetry and I continue to explore this path ahead.

ABOUT THE AUTHOR

Celina is a poet and a clinical trial manager. Having faced trauma from a young age, she started out exploring her experiences with the creative outlet of poetry and, majored in Psychology and Anthropology in her attempts to rationally understand the human experience. Her poem on her experiences as an Indian woman in Singapore was published in the country's leading gender equality advocacy group's anthology, AWARE's *What We Inherit: Growing Up Indian.* She lives with her two guinea pigs who like to ask her to get food for them instead when she's sitting around scribbling.